FROM THE EDITORS

ISSUE 04

Dear Book-lovers,

It's incredible to think that less than a year ago, Book World Magazine had just begun. What started as an idea between two best friends has grown into something we care about deeply, and we are so grateful for the support of this amazing book-loving community. Every issue is a labour of love, a testament to the countless hours, late nights, and endless conversations that go into bringing it to life.

This issue in particular holds a special place in our hearts. It all started when we stumbled upon Montgomery & Taggert, Connecticut's first romance bookstore. A bookshop dedicated entirely to romance, built by two best friends who turned their love of books into something real. We instantly saw ourselves in their story. Book World Magazine was built on the same foundation—two best friends taking a chance, creating something for the bookish world. And we realised that friendship is a thread woven throughout this issue.

From The Two Bookends, who remind us how stories deepen lifelong friendships, to Onyx Storm, which sparked bookish connections around the world, this issue is a celebration of the way books bring people together.

And then there's the Fireside Book Club. We dare you to read their story without tearing up—because we can't. This isn't just a book club; it's a legacy, a testament to the power of stories that hold people together through time, distance, and even loss. It's everything a book club should be, and we are honored to share it with you.

As we step further into 2025, we're more excited than ever about what's ahead for Book World Magazine and Book World Club. There's so much more to come, and we're so glad to have you along for the ride.

Now, grab a cup of tea if you're joining Alana, or a glass of wine if you're with Lauren, find a cosy spot, and dive into this issue. We hope you love reading it as much as we loved creating it.

Lauren Illguth
&
Alana Johnson

AMY TINTERA - LISTEN FOR THE LIE

A MUST-READ MYSTERY

ALANA AND I STARTED THE YEAR STRONG, FLYING THROUGH SOME INCREDIBLE BOOKS, BUT WE CAN ALREADY HONESTLY SAY, THIS ONE IS GOING TO BE ONE OF THE HARDEST TO BEAT.

WE HIGHLY RECOMMEND THE AUDIOBOOK FOR THIS ONE, **LISTEN FOR THE LIE** JUST WON THE 2025 AUDIE AWARD FOR BEST MYSTERY, WITH NARRATORS JANUARY LAVOY AND WILL DAMRON DELIVERING A PERFORMANCE THAT MAKES THE STORY EVEN MORE CAPITVATING.

THE NOVEL FOLLOWS LUCY CHASE, FOUND COVERED IN BLOOD AFTER HER BEST FRIEND SAVANNAH WAS MURDERED. WITH NO MEMORY OF WHAT HAPPENED SHE WAS NEVER CHARGED—BUT FIVE YEARS LATER, A TRUE CRIME PODCAST IS REOPENING THE CASE, FORCING LUCY TO CONFRONT SECRETS SHE'S TRIED TO FORGET.

AMY TINTERA DELIVERS A GRIPPING, DARKLY FUNNY, AND UNPREDICTABLE STORY THAT KEEPS YOU SECOND-GUESSING UNTIL THE VERY LAST PAGE. IF YOU LOVE MYSTERIES WITH A SIDE OF DARK HUMOR, THIS ONE IS A MUST-READ.

4 Montgomery & Taggert
A Bookstore Straightout of a Love Story

6 The Onyx Storm Phenomenon
A Book Release Like No Other

9 Readers Retreat
Onyx Storm Style

13 Emma Grey
Author Spotlight

19 Kirsten Tibballs
Queen of Chocolate

22 Street Libraries
Where Books Go to Be Found Not Forgotten

26 Allie Martina
Inside the Booth

30 Your Story Enchanted
The Magic of Bookish Candles & More

32 Victoria Wilder
A Name to Know

35 The Book That Brings You Back
Feature Article

36 Book Review
In Conversation with Jo Dixon

40 Two Bookends
Book Besties You Didn't Know You Needed

44 Penny For Your Thoughts
Young Adult Review

46 Reader Profile
@Nikita.bookshelf

50 Fireside Stories
The Fireside Family Book Club That Has Become a Legacy

MONTGOMERY & TAGGERT

A BOOKSTORE STRAIGHT OUT OF A LOVE STORY

A cozy bookstore tucked between Chester Creek and Main Street, Montgomery and Taggert isn't just Connecticut's first romance bookstore; it's a dreamlike escape for romance readers. The moment I saw it online, I knew it had to be the cover of Issue 4 of **Book World Magazine**. With its fairytale setting and connection to the community, it looks like it belongs in the very novels it sells.

Elizabeth and Sarah, best friends turned business partners, took a chance on their dream, transforming a charming historic building into something special. With its leafy courtyard, inviting shelves, and an atmosphere that radiates warmth, Montgomery and Taggert has become more than just a bookstore, it's a gathering place.

Named after the beloved families in Jude Deveraux's classic romance novels, and just like those stories, it's all about passion both for books and for building a community where romance-lovers can spend time, discover new authors, buy their next great read, and celebrate the popular genre.

Step inside, and you'll find an enchanting selection of historical, paranormal, contemporary, and fantasy romance, plus dedicated L.G.B.T.Q. shelves and even a touch of nonfiction. Every detail, from the warm, inviting decor to the personal recommendations, makes it clear that this is a bookshop made by romance fans, for romance fans.

But here's where it gets even better: if you don't want to leave, you don't have to. The second floor of this dreamy little bookshop is home to an Airbnb, offering readers and writers the perfect retreat. Imagine waking up to the smell of fresh coffee, spending the day exploring Chester Village, then curling up with a romance novel in a cozy reading nook above a bookstore. Honestly, what could be more perfect?

Montgomery and Taggert has quickly become a beloved fixture in Connecticut, especially with glimpses of snow-covered mornings adding to its charm. Their Instagram feed is a mix of cozy bookshop magic and New England beauty, making us want to grab a book, a blanket, and a cup of tea. But beyond its inviting aesthetic, this bookstore is truly rooted in its community. From hosting book clubs and author events to creating a welcoming space for romance readers, Montgomery and Taggert is a place where readers feel at home.

We couldn't be more thrilled to feature Montgomery and Taggert on the cover of this issue.

The rise of romance bookstores is something we absolutely love, and this one is pure magic.

To Elizabeth and Sarah—thank you for bringing this vision to life and for sharing it with all of us.

If you're ever in Connecticut, you know where to go for your next bookish escape.

Follow their story or check them out online @montgomeryandtaggert

www.montgomeryandtaggert.com

The Onyx Storm Phenomenon

A Book Release Like No Other

Avid Reader, West End, Brisbane

- 1997: *Avid Reader* was founded in Brisbane's West End by Fiona Stager, Kevin Guy, Verdi Guy, and Colleen Mullin.

- 2004: Moved to 193 Boundary Street, expanding its event space.

- 2015: Opened *Where the Wild Things Are,* a children's bookstore right next door.

- 2021: Won Australian Bookshop of the Year at the ABIA Awards.

Avid Reader's *Midnight Launch*

It doesn't matter what genre you prefer—if books have infiltrated your social media feed, you knew that January 21, 2025, marked the release of *Onyx Storm*. This third instalment in Rebecca Yarros's Empyrean series didn't just meet expectations; it shattered them, selling 2.7 million copies in its first week and becoming the fastest-selling adult novel in two decades.

Onyx Storm wasn't just a book release—it was a global event. Midnight launches took place around the world, with bookstores packed and fans eager to get their hands on a copy the moment the clock struck twelve. Being in Australia, we were among the first readers in the world to get our hands on the book, and we chose to celebrate at one of Brisbane's most beloved independent bookstores: *Avid Reader*.

The midnight release night at *Avid Reader* was transformed into a haven for fans. By 9:30 p.m., a line had already snaked up the street and around the corner, buzzing with excitement. Some attendees arrived in costume, embodying characters from the series, while others eagerly chatted about their theories and expectations.

Once inside, guests were welcomed into the bookstore's courtyard and verandah, where the evening kicked off with book reviews by the passionate and knowledgeable *Avid Reader* staff. *Fourth Wing*-inspired cocktails were available for purchase, fueling the lively atmosphere. Conversations about the series filled every corner, voices overlapping in excited debates and laughter. The noise level? Let's just say it was impossible to miss—the kind of buzz only passionate readers can create.

The absolute highlight of the night was a challenging *Fourth Wing* and *Iron Flame* trivia quiz, which had everyone engaged, shouting answers, and cheering for the winners, who walked away with a collection of prizes.

The best-dressed contest brought even more excitement, with one standout winner—a young woman clad in an intricately crafted rider's leather outfit, complete with braided hair, strapped daggers, and leather arm guards. Her dedication to the look was nothing short of impressive.

As the clock neared midnight, everyone lined up once more, ready for the final countdown. Everyone in the bookstore erupted in cheers as the boxes of books were finally opened at 11:59 p.m. and fans were allowed to buy at the stroke of midnight. Fans clutched their copies with a mix of excitement and anticipation, some immediately posing for photos, while others simply held their book close, savouring the moment. *Avid Reader* had even sent out an email earlier that day to their waiting list of over 120 people, inviting them to come by after midnight to purchase a copy. Some arrived in pyjamas, eager to get their hands on the book, proving just how monumental this release was.

We were incredibly grateful to be able to cover this event and be part of such a spectacular night. We reached out to Avid Reader to attend, and they welcomed us with open arms.

The energy, the enthusiasm, and the passion of everyone in attendance made it a night not to be forgotten. We made so many wonderful connections, and the atmosphere was nothing short of brilliant. *Avid Reader* did an incredible job organising the night, and we can't wait to attend more of their events in the future.

Avid Reader Brisbane *Onyx Storm* **Midnight Launch**

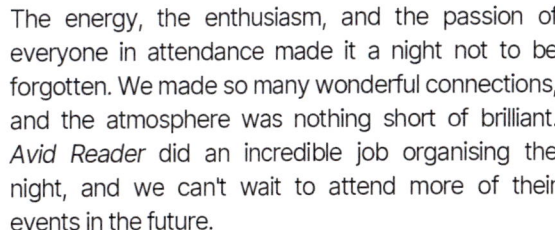

The Global Frenzy of *Onyx Storm*

The world went a little dragon crazy in the lead-up to *Onyx Storm*.

It wasn't just social media hyping the release, it was everywhere. Murals of the Empyrean series' book covers were splashed across giant city walls in three of Australia's biggest capitals. *Onyx Storm* even took over Times Square in New York City, its glowing cover looming over thousands of people. Special editions disappeared in seconds, and fans were collecting every possible version, as if stocking up for war. By the time release day hit, it felt like the entire world had a dragon on their mind.

And with that came one unbreakable rule: No spoilers. This wasn't just a courtesy, it was a matter of honor. For at least two weeks, readers prefaced every post with a dramatic warning, giving others just enough time to scroll away before potential devastation. Even now, a month later, new readers dodge spoilers like riders dodging venin, scrolling past posts with Basgiath-level reflexes.

Meanwhile, Rebecca Yarros has come under more scrutiny than Donald Trump at a press conference. Every interview, every panel appearance, every casual remark is dissected, analyzed, and turned into a full-blown theory. Did she pause for half a second before answering a question? That must mean something. Did she blink twice when someone mentioned Xaden? Definitely a clue. At this point, Rebecca probably has to think through every word she says, knowing that somewhere, someone is already drafting a ten-slides Instagram breakdown on it.

And with the next book not expected until 2027, fans have nothing but time to theorize. The *Onyx Storm* phenomenon isn't dying down, it's just getting more unhinged.

Reader's Retreat
Onyx Storm Style

After the worldwide release of *Onyx Storm*, this wasn't just a book people read—it was a book people experienced. Across the globe, fans gathered for book retreats, making it clear that this series had transcended the page.

For us, this was more than just a weekend getaway—it was the launch of our company's new reading retreats, designed to bring book lovers together in unforgettable settings. And what better way to start than with one of the biggest fantasy releases in years?

We hosted our *Onyx Storm* retreat on the Gold Coast, Queensland, Australia, at the stunning InterContinental Sanctuary Cove. The weather was ideal, the setting was beautiful, the atmosphere exactly what we had envisioned—a space for readers to unwind, connect, and dive deeper into the book they loved.

But this was just the beginning.

What if you could escape for a weekend and the only thing you had to do was read?
No cooking, no planning, no worrying about schedules. Just you, your book, and a group of like-minded readers in a breathtaking setting.

That's exactly what Book World Club Retreats are designed to offer. Whether it's a luxurious hotel, a charming winery, or a private house by the coast, each retreat will give every book-lover the space to relax, recharge, and connect. Picture mornings spent sipping coffee on the verandah, afternoons discussing your favorite books over wine, and evenings unwinding by the fire with a novel in hand and an author at the table.

Throughout our *Onyx Storm* weekend, guests enjoyed cocktails by the pool, intimate book discussions, a beautifully set dinner with personalized gift bags, and a lively game inspired by our book club guide. Laughter and deep conversations filled every moment, from spirited theory debates at the pool bar to a final morning sharing favorite reads and discovering new book recommendations.

From the moment guests arrived at our first retreat, the stress of daily life melted away. They settled into the rhythm of an experience curated for them—where the only agenda was to indulge in their love of books. The friendships formed that weekend continue to grow, with our retreat's Instagram chat still buzzing daily.

Now, we're bringing that magic to more readers. With future retreats already in the works—including author-led getaways, wine country escapes, and destination retreats—this is your chance to experience the ultimate book-lover's getaway.

If you've ever dreamed of stepping away from the chaos and into a world where reading is the only priority, Book World Club Retreats are waiting for you.

Where will we take you next?

Nicole
The BookLoveAholic Behind the Buzz, Theories & Bookish Fun

Among the incredible attendees was Nicole, a passionate fantasy and romantasy 'book-stagrammer' whose love for the *Fourth Wing* series is undeniable. Nicole has built a name for herself in the bookish community, interviewing authors on her podcast, Romantasy Readers, sharing in-depth theories, and connecting readers through her engaging Instagram at @bookloveaholic.

Nicole's bookish journey didn't start with *Fourth Wing,* but it was the book that changed everything for her. Having grown up on *Twilight, Vampire Academy*, and *True Blood*, she always loved fantasy, but life got in the way. After a decade-long reading slump, she picked up *Crescent City* by Sarah J. Maas and was immediately pulled back into the world of books. From there, she devoured *Throne of Glass*, *ACOTAR*, and a growing list of romantasy favorites. But when *Fourth Wing* dropped, something clicked.

She couldn't stop theorizing and she wanted—needed—to share those thoughts. That's when she started her Instagram account, hoping to find a handful of people to geek out with (her words.) Now, with nearly 25,000 followers, publishers reaching out, and a podcast where she gets to chat with authors, Nicole has become a go-to name in the romantasy space.

At the retreat, Nicole led a Theories at the Pool Bar session, helping dissect every possible outcome for the series and sparking discussions that had everyone questioning what they thought they knew. She also hosted an impromptu trivia session on the final morning, bringing even more fun (and competition) to the weekend. But beyond that, she was a catalyst for deeper conversations—whether it was about the rise of romantasy, the art of book theorizing, or the challenges of being an Australian bookstagrammer in an U.S.-dominated market.

Her passion for books goes beyond just reading. She's fascinated by the craft of storytelling, the different ways authors build worlds, and the impact books can have on readers. She's interviewed authors like Pen Cole —*Spark of the Everflame* —getting insight into their creative processes and the pressures of delivering anticipated books. She also keeps a pulse on the book industry, noticing trends like the rise of indie authors, the growing market for special edition books, and the way independent bookstores thrive when they build a strong reading community.

Nicole isn't just reading books, she's helping shape the conversation around them. Whether she's breaking down a theory, reviewing a new release, or simply sharing her latest bookish obsession, she brings an energy that makes people excited to be part of the romantasy world. Nicole is still navigating where her bookish journey will take her, whether it's expanding her podcast, diving into writing, or continuing to build her brand, one thing is certain: her impact on the romantasy community is only growing.

As the retreat came to a close, we left with more than just memories. *Onyx Storm* **gave us the perfect excuse to gather, celebrate, and connect over our shared love for books. But beyond that, it reinforced the power of fandom—the way a single story can bring people together, ignite conversations, and forge lasting friendships.**

And as we all wait (impatiently) for the next book, one thing is clear: the *Onyx Storm* **phenomenon isn't fading anytime soon. If anything, it's only just beginning.**

EMMA GREY
Author Spotlight

Emma Grey's Moment Has Arrived And She's Earned Every Bit Of It

For many, Emma Grey might seem like an "overnight success." In reality, her journey to becoming a bestselling author spans nearly four decades of perseverance, rejection, and a commitment to storytelling. In our conversation, Emma shared insights into her whirlwind experiences, unexpected creative ventures, and the emotional depth that fuels her novels.

Her novel *The Last Love Note* catapulted her into the global spotlight. This deeply personal story, inspired by the loss of her husband, resonated with readers worldwide, leading to features in Book of the Month, *Oprah Daily*, and *The Washington Post*. It also marked her U.S. debut, with her books now available in Target stores across America, a significant achievement for an Australian author.

However, this success did not happen overnight.

> *People act like I just wrote my first book and everything fell into place,"* she said with a laugh. *"But I've been writing since I was fourteen. That's thirty-eight years.*

Emma's publishing journey began in 2005 with *Wits' End Before Breakfast! Confessions of a Working Mum*. She later authored Y.A. novels, including *Unrequited*, which was adapted into a musical, and co-authored a self-help book with Audrey Thomas entitled *I Don't Have Time*, all the while regularly writing for major Australian publications.

She spent years as a columnist for *Her Canberra* and contributed to *The Age* and *The Sydney Morning Herald*.

Despite her extensive portfolio, it's only recently that Emma has been able to write full-time. *"For years, I was squeezing writing around full-time jobs and single parenting three kids after my husband Jeff passed away,"* she said.

"The eight years since Jeff died have been a marathon of exhaustion, but persistence is the secret of success."

Her most recent novel, *Pictures of You*, delves into coercive control and the complexities of abusive relationships. This work was influenced by her daughter, Hannah, a criminology doctoral candidate specialising in gendered violence.

At the Australian Embassy in Washington, D.C., Emma had the unique opportunity to share the stage with Hannah. *"She's doing a Ph.D. in criminology, specializing in gendered violence, and to hear her speak alongside me was a moment I'll always treasure,"* Emma said. It was a rare chance for mother and daughter to discuss the themes that underpin *Pictures of You*.

The novel has sparked profound conversations with survivors and advocates. Readers have reached out, sharing how the book reshaped their perspectives on past relationships.

These personal connections, the real conversations she has with readers, mean more to her than anything. Emma isn't just a writer who puts books into the world, she actively engages with her audience, spending time online talking to people, answering questions, and listening to their stories. At an event in Charleston, an entire book club attended after previously connecting with Emma over Zoom.

> **❝** *It's not just about selling books. It's about people feeling seen.* **❞**

Emma's resilience is evident in her approach to rejection. Inspired by an article about a writer aiming for 100 rejections annually to reframe failure as progress, she adopted this mindset. Now, she tracks her rejections on a chart in her kitchen, setting a yearly goal of 100.

"Rejection isn't failure, it means you're trying. I even got a rejection from a big Hollywood studio the other day, and I was thrilled because it meant I was leveling up," she explained. She believes that too many brilliant manuscripts remain unpublished because authors give up too soon. *"I always remind writers: just because you've been turned down doesn't mean your book isn't worthy. It just hasn't found the right person yet."*

This persistence has led Emma's career in unexpected directions, including a musical adaptation of her Y.A. novel *Unrequited*. Originally written for her daughter Sophie, who hated reading but loved Harry Styles, the story evolved into a musical with composer Sally Whitwell. *"It's basically Pride and Prejudice, but with boy bands,"* Emma said with a laugh.

The musical's performance at Sophie's school, just a year after Jeff's passing, was a beacon during a dark time. *"Being surrounded by teenage theatre kids, disco balls, and glitter cannons; it was a light in the darkness."* Emma hopes to see it performed again, and interest from schools is growing.

Her creative ambitions now extend to screenwriting. *"I'd love to move into screenwriting,"* she said. *"I even have a Hallmark Christmas movie idea mapped out, which is funny because I never outline my books, but I have this movie fully plotted."* Unlike her usual spontaneous writing process, this project is meticulously planned.

Pictures of You and *The Last Love Note* have attracted the attention of T.V. and film producers opening new doors for Emma's storytelling. Having already seen her Y.A. novel *Unrequited* adapted into a musical, she understands how stories evolve across different mediums. *"A story changes when it moves to another format, and I'm okay with that. As long as the heart of it stays intact."*

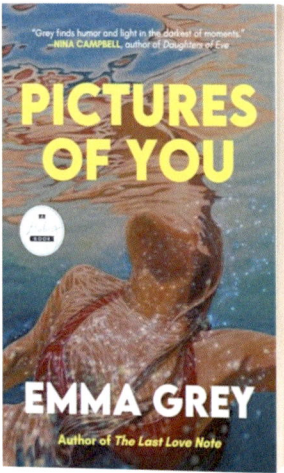

Beyond writing, Emma has embraced photography as a cherished hobby. She discovered this passion during the Covid-19 pandemic after her husband Jeff's passing.

"I did an online course on how to use your phone camera to get better pictures, and then I graduated to a big camera," she shared. *"It is literally the only activity I ever do that really takes me away from the entire world."*

Photography became a therapeutic escape, allowing her to immerse herself fully and momentarily forget the challenges she was facing.

"There were times during the pandemic where I'd go out for a little hour-a-day wander, and I would find myself on the ground with the camera, with a macro lens, trying to capture a sunburst on a dew drop on a blade of grass," Emma recalled. *"I'd look up at the end of the hour, having forgotten there was a pandemic."*

Looking ahead, Emma's next novel, *Start at the End* is slated for publication in the U.S. with Zibby Publishing, U.K. and Australia in 2026. Like *Pictures of You*, it is an ambitious concept that pushes structural boundaries. Emma says, *"I love playing with timelines, perspective, and high-concept hooks."*

Reflecting on her journey, she mused,
*"It took me thirty-eight years to become
an overnight success
but I wouldn't change a thing."*

Checkout more of Emma's amazing photos @emmagreyphotography

BOOK CLUB QUIZ

At **Book World Club**, we're starting the year with a literature themed quiz, perfect for sparking some friendly competition at your next book club meeting! Try it out with your group, and award a fun little prize to the winner. Find all the answers at bookworldmagazine.com/quiz-answers.

What bestselling contemporary novel features a woman who rides the same train every day and becomes obsessed with a couple she sees from the window?

Which famous classic novel has been adapted into the most movies and T.V. shows?

In which bestselling novel would you find the phrase: "I am haunted by humans"?

What is the term for a book that tells a story within a story?

Which audiobook platform was acquired by Amazon in 2008?

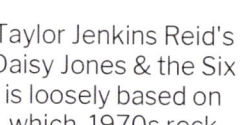

Taylor Jenkins Reid's Daisy Jones & the Six is loosely based on which 1970s rock band?

In Tomorrow, and Tomorrow, and Tomorrow, what is the main character's profession?

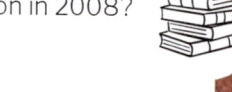

Which novel ends with, "And so, as Tiny Tim observed, God bless Us, Every One!"?

Who holds the record for the most romance novels published?

What book opens with "You better not never tell nobody but God"?

A Man Called Ove was written by which author?

What is the pen name of Samuel Clemens?

What is the name of Amazon's self-publishing platform?

Which George Orwell novella is being adapted into an animated film directed by Andy Serkis, scheduled for release in 2025?

What classic novel was banned in the U.S. for its "indecent" content when first published in 1928?

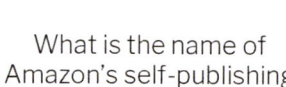
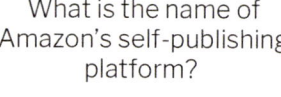

If you're making a chocolate cake for book club, why not get a recipe from the best? **Kirsten Tibballs** isn't just any pastry chef, she's the **Queen of Chocolate.**

One of Australia's most celebrated chocolatiers, she's trained with the best in Paris and Brussels, won gold at the Pastry Olympics, and holds the highest-ever score for handmade chocolates at the World Pastry Team Championships. She's the founder of the **Savour Chocolate and Patisserie School,** a global ambassador for Callebaut, and the mastermind behind some of MasterChef Australia's most legendary pressure tests.

Kirsten's passion for pastry has made her an international sensation, with her hit T.V. show **The Chocolate Queen** airing in over 40 countries and three cookbooks under her belt. Whether she's crafting world-class confections or teaching home bakers how to master the perfect ganache, she does it all with a flair that's both awe-inspiring and approachable.

Since **Onyx Storm** has taken over the book world and features a memorable chocolate cake moment, it felt right to celebrate with a recipe of our own, one created by the best. Because if there's one thing book lovers can agree on, it's that chocolate and a good story are the perfect pairing.

Decadent Six-layer Chocolate Cake

by Kirsten Tibballs

Serves: 12-15.

Chocolate Cake

Ingredients:

vegetable oil spray, for greasing;
240 g (15 oz) plain (all-purpose) flour;
105 g (3 ½ oz) dutch-processed cocoa powder;
15 g (½ oz) bicarbonate of soda (baking soda);
1 teaspoon baking powder;
420 g (15 oz) caster (superfine sugar);
1 teaspoon salt;
115 ml (3 ¾ fl oz) coconut oil or vegetable oil;
100 g (3 ½ oz) whole eggs;
120 ml (4 fl oz) buttermilk;
1 teaspoon vanilla bean paste; and
120 ml (4 fl oz) hot water.

Method:

Preheat the oven to 150°C (300°F.) Grease two 18cm (7 inch) round cake tins with vegetable oil spray, then line them with baking paper;

Sift the flour, cocoa powder, bicarbonate of soda, and baking powder into a bowl, add the sugar and salt, then set aside;

In a stand mixer with a whisk attachment, beat the coconut oil, eggs, buttermilk and vanilla for one minute;

Add the dry ingredients and mix until just combined and while mixing, slowly add the hot water in a continuous stream;

Divide the batter evenly between the two prepared cake tins, then bake for 50-55 minutes, until a skewer inserted into the centre comes out clean;

Leave to cool at room temperature before placing in the freezer for a minimum of one hour; and

Using a serrated knife, trim the tops off the chilled cakes, then slice each cake into three equal layers and set aside.

Note:
To make your own buttermilk, combine 120 ml (4 fl oz) of full-cream milk with 1 tsp of fresh lemon juice and leave to stand for five minutes before using.

Decadent Chocolate Ganache

Ingredients:

540 ml (18 ½ fl oz) thickened (whipping) cream;
1 teaspoon vanilla bean paste;
60 g (2 ¼ oz) liquid glucose; and
1.14 kg (2 lb 8 oz) good-quality milk chocolate.

Method:

Combine the cream, vanilla, and glucose in a saucepan over medium heat and bring to the boil;

Meanwhile, place the chocolate in a microwave-safe plastic bowl and heat in the microwave on high in 30-second increments until it is 50% melted;

Pour the hot cream mixture over the chocolate and whisk until the chocolate is completely melted and incorporated; and

Cover with plastic wrap touching the surface of the ganache and leave to sit at room temperature for approximately three hours, until it is firm but still spreadable.

Chocolate Soak

Ingredients:

100 ml (3 ½ fl oz) water;
100 g (3 ½ oz) caster (superfine) sugar;
1 teaspoon vanilla bean paste; and
1 tablespoon dutch-processed cocoa powder.

Method:

Combine the water, sugar, and vanilla in a saucepan over high heat and bring to the boil; and

Once the sugar has completely dissolved, remove from the heat, add the cocoa powder and whisk until there are no lumps remaining and set aside to cool completely at room temperature.

Milk Chocolate Curls

Ingredients:

250 g (9 oz) good-quality milk chocolate.

Method:

Temper the chocolate by placing it in a microwave-safe plastic bowl and heat it in the microwave on high in 30-second increments, stirring in between and once you have 50% solids and 50% liquid, stir vigorously until the solids have completely melted;

If you have some resistant buttons, gently heat the chocolate with a hair dryer, while stirring, until melted;

Spread a small amount of the tempered chocolate in a thin layer over a stone or smooth cold work surface;

Work the chocolate backwards and forwards with an offset palette knife just until it begins to go dull;

Using a metal scraper, or the blade of a knife, scrape the chocolate to create different-shaped curls; and

Leave to set at room temperature.

Assembly

Photography by Armelle Habib

Method:

Place the first layer of chocolate cake on a serving plate and using a pastry brush, brush the surface of the cake generously with the chocolate soak;

Spread one-sixth of the ganache over the cake, pushing it towards the edges;

Repeat with the remaining chocolate cake layers, chocolate soak, and ganache;

Top the finished cake with the chocolate curls; and

The cake can be stored in the fridge for up to five days and leave it to come back to room temperature before serving.

For best results:

To create even layers, make marks around the cake where you will cut it, and cut while turning the cake until you reach the centre;

Once you have cut the cake into layers, return them to the freezer to make handling and assembling easier;

Use one of the cake bases, base facing upwards, as the top layer of the cake and this will ensure a flat surface on top; and

Don't let the ganache become too firm before layering the cake.

Next level:

You can dust the chocolate curls with edible gold lustre dust.

Suzie - Hartree Corner Street Library

STREET LIBRARIES

Where Books Go To Be Found Not Forgotten

The inspiration for this article came from Suzie at Hartree Corner Street Library.

I've always believed street libraries are something special. They bring communities together, create unexpected bookish connections, and give stories a second life. But I wanted to explore them in a way that goes beyond the usual narrative.

When, Suzie shared a thought that truly resonated with me:

"Street libraries are no longer a place to dump unwanted books. They are a launching pad of incredible ideas."

That one sentence reframed everything for me. Street libraries aren't just about books, they're about discovery, about passing stories forward, about sharing something meaningful.

So, thank you, Suzie, this article is my way of honouring that idea.

Across the world, small, wooden boxes filled with books are changing the way communities engage with stories. Street libraries, little free libraries, community bookshelves, whatever you call them, these free book exchanges have become a grassroots movement that brings people together, fosters a love of reading, and provides access to books for those who might not otherwise have them. But there's something we need to talk about... What's going inside these libraries?

Sadly, sometimes these beautiful community resources become dumping grounds for unwanted, damaged, or neglected titles that few would pick up in a bookstore. That's not what street libraries are about. They should be stocked and many are with books that spark curiosity, books that inspire, books that people genuinely want to read. It's time to change the way we think about what we give.

According to the streetlibrary.org.au website the idea behind street libraries is simple. Take a book, give a book, and share a book. In greater Sydney, Australia alone there is estimated to be around two thousand little libraries. But in some places, this simple idea becomes a lifeline. In many communities, particularly in low-income areas or remote regions, public libraries are scarce and bookstores are a luxury. For some, street libraries are the only way to access books for free. That makes it even more important to think about what we donate.

When we fill these little libraries with books we love, stories that have shaped us, books by incredible authors, especially indie authors who don't always get shelf space in traditional libraries. We're not just giving away a book, we're introducing someone to a new world, a new perspective, a new favorite author. Street libraries bridge gaps between generations, between neighbors, between those who have access to books and those who don't, but only if we treat them as places of discovery, not disposal.

One of the most exciting opportunities street libraries offer is a way to introduce indie authors to readers who might never find them otherwise. Over 70% of books in public libraries and major bookstores come from traditional publishers, leaving indie books

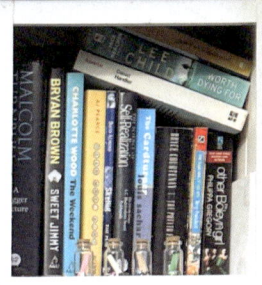

fighting for visibility. That's where we come in. By donating a book you've written or an indie book you've loved, you're helping bring diverse, fresh voices into the community. You're giving someone the chance to discover something new, something different, something they might never have picked up otherwise. The same goes for books from second-hand stores and independent bookstores, giving them new life in a street library is a powerful way to support authors, small businesses, and sustainability all at once.

Because street libraries are not where books go to be forgotten, they're where books go to be found.

Serendipitous Sunday
and The Hulk – Evatt Street Library

The Hulk – Evatt Street Library isn't just a book exchange; it's a community treasure. Established in 2018 by Neill Taylor, this bright green street library stands out in Evatt, A.C.T., fostering unexpected moments of joy and connection.

One evening, a message arrived from the Netherlands. A woman wanted to surprise her nine-year-old niece in Evatt with her favorite books, Anne of Green Gables, but she needed help getting them there. The Hulk didn't have the books, but within 24 hours, thanks to the Canberra street library and Buy Nothing networks, three copies were in hand.

That Sunday, Little Miss Nine and her family arrived, beaming with excitement. Sharing how the books had traveled across the globe made the moment even more special. A simple request turned into a heartwarming connection—one that proves street libraries are more than just shelves of books.

Neill Taylor's creation, The Hulk, continues to bring people together in ways no one could have expected. A reminder that you never know how a street library can brighten someone's day.

A Fairy's Wish
Montgomery Drive Park Little Library

When Edna Searle downsized in retirement, she dreamed of sharing her love of books with a Little Library in her front yard. But living in a cul-de-sac wasn't ideal for foot traffic, so she reached out to her local councillor over a cup of tea. The idea? A community street library in the local parklands, a place where families gathered for barbecues and playground adventures.

The councillor wasted no time. The Alexandra Hills Men's Shed built the library, and a local youth worker, once a graffiti artist—painted a mural on the park's amenities block, where the library would be mounted. Over a weekend, families watched in fascination as the artwork came to life. But one little girl had a special request: Where's the fairy? So, the artist returned and added a fairy to the scene, because every magical place deserves a touch of whimsy

Now, the Montgomery Drive Park Little Library is a beloved part of the community. Once books have been read and shared locally, they are repurposed and sent to regional areas, continuing their journey to places like Bogan Gate, Rathdowney, and Molong.

A street library isn't just about books, it's about connection, kindness, and sometimes, a little bit of magic.

From A Little Library
To Lifelong Friendships

When I started my own street library in 2022, I never imagined I would meet so many amazing people. I had always thought I might catch a glimpse of someone using the library while leaving the house or checking the mailbox, but what I have ended up with has exceeded all my expectations.

Within a few days of setting up my library I put a post on a local Facebook community page notifying people in the area what a street library is and how it works. Within the first 24 hours I had my first visitor who dropped off three to four books, and in the next few weeks I had a $20 cafe gift voucher left in my donation box. No name was left, but it blew me away that someone would be so generous to a stranger.

My eldest son started school the next year. I went to the Outside Hours School Care (O.H.S.C.) facility and got talking to the coordinator there. The conversation soon turned to books, and we worked out it was her who was not only my first visitor, but left the $20 gift voucher!

Over the next few months, I finally plucked up the courage to invite her to join my book club. It wasn't until she left the O.H.S.C. facility that our professional customer/staff relationship faded, and we became true friends. Over the last couple of years, alongside a few other book club ladies, our friendship has blossomed. We've attended book events, dinners, movie nights, and road trips, and even celebrated Christmas with secret Santa.

I'm so grateful for the wonderful group of women I can now call dear friends, all because of a vintage cabinet full of books that I placed in my front yard.

Rebecca Damsma

You can follow Bec's new library setup in the Whitsundays via @becandthebooks on Instagram, or check out her old library posts for inspiration using #beaumontctstreetlibrary.

A GLOBAL CHALLENGE

Thanks Author M.L. Jewel for starting us off.

Donate Like You're Handpicking A Gift For A Friend

At Book World Magazine, we're not just talking about it, we're doing it.

We've been buying books from independent bookstores, second-hand shops, and indie authors to donate to street libraries around Australia. Now, we're challenging readers, authors, and book-lovers around the world to do the same.

- 📖 Find a book you love, one that truly meant something to you.
- 📝 Write a note inside. Tell the next reader why you loved it or what makes it special.
- 📍 Place it in a street library (or free library) near you. 📷 Snap a photo and share it!

We would love to see this movement spread beyond Australia, into the States, across Europe, and beyond. Whether it's a little free library in the U.S., a street library in the U.K., or a community bookshelf in a local café in Paris, let's fill them with books that matter.

Join us - tag us - let's do this together.

If you donate a book to a street library, tag us! We'll be sharing stories, photos, and posts about this movement in the next issue of Book World Magazine.

GIVE A BOOK A NEW BEGINNING, BECAUSE EVERY STORY DESERVES A NEXT CHAPTER.

Inside The Booth with
Allie Martina

For audiobook lovers, narrators are more than just voices, they're the unseen storytellers who can breathe life into a book, elevating great stories and making even the simplest moments unforgettable. In this issue of Inside The Booth, we sit down with Allie Martina, a narrator who has quickly made her mark in the romance genre. From her journey into voice work to the stories that have shaped her, we get to know the person behind the mic and the passion that fuels her storytelling.

"La Petite Elva"
Photo Provided by Allie Martina

Hey Allie, let's start simple, who are you? What's your story so far, and what led you into the world of audiobook narration?

That's actually a hard question. Who am I? It depends on what project I'm working on. In the audiobook world, I'm best known as Allie Martina, the pseudonym I use whenever I narrate romance novels. Honestly, that's been my primary career focus in the last few years, and I love it!

As far as my acting goes, I've been at it since high school, starting with on-camera commercials. As a college student, I majored in theater arts, then went on to act in local plays. Ultimately, I found my home behind the microphone and fell in love with voice acting. I've pretty much done it all within the world of voice-over and narration, spanning over three decades. I suppose what led me to audiobook narration specifically was the desire to get back to my theater roots, where I could voice different characters and be part of a story from beginning to end.

It's interesting to note that when you asked me who I am, my first instinct was to rattle off specific credits from my career. But honestly, those credits mean less and less to me these days (and they would probably bore you.) I think what makes me who I am is more about my values than what I've done as an actor. I value family, authenticity, connection, and humor. That last one is important because life gets hard, and there's nothing like a good laugh to bring some levity to a situation. These values are a big part of what makes me who I am.

Has storytelling always been a big part of your life, whether through books, film, or other media? And if so, was there a particular story, book, or experience that made a lasting impression on you?

There are many wonderful storytellers in my family, but perhaps the best of all was my Grandma Robley. Her stories were always lively and entertaining, as she believed that even the best stories deserved embellishments to make them even better. I vividly remember her telling marvelous stories of my ancestors, many of whom were Vaudeville performers in the early 1900s.

The wild stories of them traveling on trains, performing from city to city in dusty theaters on the circuit, would captivate me and take me to a completely different world, one where women were fearless and a bit eccentric. These stories also fueled my interest in acting from a very young age. In fact, I have wanted to be a performer for as long as I can remember.

What's one thing you've learned about yourself since becoming a narrator?

I've learned that there are a few ordinary words that I've confidently mispronounced for decades. It took audiobook proofers to bring these words to my attention, and I'm grateful for it. Narration has definitely broadened my vocabulary, too. Sorry, that was two things, wasn't it?

Allie Martina's ancestors, early 1900s Vaudeville performers

La Petite Elva

Audiobook narration requires focus and endurance. Do you have any rituals or tips for preparing to perform?

I don't have any fancy rituals beyond quickly warming up my body and voice, as well as staying hydrated. I also keep myself pretty caffeinated.

You've narrated across romance sub-genres. Is there a project that's your personal favorite, and what made it so special?

The honest truth is that each story I narrate touches me in different ways. It's impossible to pick a favorite.

That said, **Gravity** by Sara Cate is one of my favorites. It's packed full of angst, emotion, and turmoil, which made it both challenging and fun to perform. **Gravity** also has the best love scene I've ever narrated, which happens to take place on a private helicopter.

Another book that really captured my heart is **The Mix-Up** by Eve Marian. I found myself rooting for the female protagonist and celebrating each moment of personal growth as she built a new life for herself after coming out of an emotionally abusive relationship. Eve Marian is a writer I wish more people knew about.

What's a genre or story you haven't narrated yet but would love to explore?

I have narrated a lot of romantic suspense, but I have not narrated any thrillers or horror stories. I would love to, though!

Not only have you recently stepped into audiobook narration, but you've also launched Zipless, a podcast where you talk to authors and narrators about audiobooks, storytelling, and romance. What inspired you to start the podcast, and what do you hope to bring to listeners?

Allie Martina and Jill Ruby
Recently fillmed at The Ripped Bodice in New York

You're right, I started narrating during Covid, which is relatively recent. I was looking for ways to supplement my voice-over income because the world of advertising was adjusting to the new social climate and shutdowns. While my narration career came about from the need to diversify my work, the idea to do a podcast felt more like a lightning strike.

Even though romance books are enormously popular, there's still a level of shame or embarrassment around reading them. I felt inspired to explore these themes on a deeper level, wanting to create something that spoke to both the mind and the heart of listeners, with the goal of normalizing women's sexuality and romantic wants and needs.

From there, I met with award-winning podcast producer Jill Ruby. We connected immediately and found that we collaborated extremely well together. It took about six months to conceptualize, start production, and begin interviewing authors. Honestly, working with Jill on Zipless has been a highlight of my life. This show is something we're both passionate about and proud of. It's been a blast to produce and host.

What are your ultimate goals for Zipless? Who's your dream guest for the show?

We definitely want to grow our audience, but we also want to maintain the personal nature of podcasting. I love the idea that I'm talking to one listener at a time while still being part of a wider podcast community.

Our dream guest? That's easy: Erica Jong. Erica is a second-wave feminist American poet and writer, and her most famous book, **Fear of Flying** (1973,)is the inspiration for the title of our series. If anyone out there is looking for a book about real women having real sex and chasing real romance, they should run out and buy **Fear of Flying!**

With book clubs on the rise, they've become such a great way to connect over stories. Are you part of one, or do you have a book bestie, someone you always swap recommendations with? And if not, would you ever join one?

I used to be in book clubs, and I love the community they bring! However, between prepping and reading books for narration and Zipless, I don't have time to read anything else.

There could be worse problems to have.

Empowerment through storytelling is something you're clearly passionate about, it's at the heart of what you do with Zipless and your narration work. What do you think is the most powerful thing about women owning their stories, whether through reading, writing, or listening?

First of all, thank you for asking such compelling (and challenging) questions.

Most wonderful stories show a journey of personal growth that draws the reader in. Sometimes books provide windows into another person's life, and sometimes they provide reflections of our own. Whether I'm narrating or hosting Zipless, I love finding those moments of empowerment and growth.

We have a segment on Zipless where listeners write in with personal experiences related to reading romance books. I've read many inspirational letters, but here are a few specific examples:

· One woman wrote in about reading **Praise** by Sara Cate and realizing she might have a praise kink herself. She felt encouraged to talk to her boyfriend about it, which led to spicing up their love life.

· Another listener felt healed by reading romance after a lifetime of repressing her sexuality due to cultural and religious beliefs. These women are claiming what they want and discovering freedom in that.

Narrators may not be the characters they portray, but their voices are what bring those characters to life. Allie Martina is proof that a great narrator is more than just a performer, they are a storyteller, a guide, and sometimes, the reason we fall in love with a book in the first place. Through her work in audiobooks and Zipless, she's shaping conversations around romance, storytelling, and the power of voice. And for audiobook fans like us, getting to know the people behind the voices makes every listen even more meaningful.

YOUR STORY ENCHANTED
THE MAGIC OF BOOKISH CANDLES & MORE

Your Story Enchanted isn't just a business, it's a portal into the heart of bookish magic, handcrafted by Tegan, a creator whose passion for books has turned into something truly special. Tegan started her journey in 2014, making candles for fun while balancing a corporate job and raising two kids. But when she merged her love for books with her talent for crafting, everything changed. "*I made things I loved, and suddenly people wanted them too!*" she says. Now, her officially licensed, handcrafted bookish candles and merchandise are adored by fans worldwide.

Her store is a treasure trove for book-lovers, featuring exclusive candles, perfumes, 3-D printed dragon eggs, and jewellery inspired by epic fantasy worlds like *Fourth Wing*, *A Court of Thorns and Roses*, *Twilight*, and *Lord of the Rings*. Her *Fourth Wing* dragon candle became so popular that readers buy one to burn and one to display, a book-lover's trophy.

But Your Story Enchanted is more than just an online shop. Tegan is one of Australia's only mobile candle workshop

providers, bringing hands-on, immersive experiences to book clubs, corporate teams, and literary events. *"Readers don't just want books, they want to live inside them,"* she says. *"That's what I create."*

Looking ahead, Tegan dreams of opening a real-life bookish haven, where visitors walk through grand archways draped in fairy lights, surrounded by the scents and sights of their favourite stories. Until then, she's expanding internationally and creating new, exclusive collections for indie authors and major bookshops.

If you're looking for one-of-a-kind, book-inspired treasures, don't wait bestsellers disappear fast!

✨ EXCLUSIVE GIVEAWAY ✨

To celebrate Your Story Enchanted, Tegan is giving away a romantasy-inspired candle! Keep an eye on our socials for details on how to enter.

📷 **Want to see more?** Follow @yourstoryenchanted on Instagram or visit www.yourstoryenchanted.com.au to shop her magical collection.

Victoria Wilder is not just an indie romance author to watch, she's an author on the rise. With an ever-growing readership, glowing reviews, and a Goodreads rating that puts her among the best in indie romance, she has now taken the leap to full-time writing. If her success so far is any indication, this is only the beginning.

Her books are smart, her heroines are sharp, and the pacing in her stories is on point. When I picked up *Bourbon & Lies*, I was immediately drawn to its striking cover, but by the final page, it wasn't the design I was thinking about, it was the writing.

After finishing, I did what any hooked reader would do: I hunted down every book Wilder had written and devoured them all. There's something about the way she tells a story, and as I soon learned, that storytelling talent has only just begun to unfold.

During our call with her, it became clear Victoria Wilder isn't just another great indie romance author. Her books aren't just good; they're the kind that stay with you long after you've turned the last page. Unlike many authors who dream of writing their entire lives, Wilder's journey to full-time authorship was anything but conventional. *"I was in my mid-30s thinking, 'When am I going to figure out what this dream is that everyone talks about?'"* she told us.

After years in marketing and public relations, she found herself searching for something that truly excited her. It wasn't until after having her son that she became immersed in romance novels, not just as a reader, but as an active participant in the book community. She launched a bookstagram, bought all the merch, and, before long, had a new thought, *"I want to write one of these."*

The Riggs Family series, a four-books saga, introduced readers to Wilder's storytelling in 2022 with her debut novel, *Peaks of Color*. With each release, her fan base grew, but it was *Bourbon & Lies* that truly marked a turning point in her career. The novel launched her **Bourbon Boys** series, following the powerful and enigmatic Fox brothers, owners of a Kentucky bourbon distillery. It drew readers into a world of high-stakes romance, family legacy, and the rich traditions of bourbon making.

Because the bourbon distillery feels like a character in itself, I was genuinely surprised to learn that Wilder didn't come from a bourbon family or have any prior connection to the industry. The way she wrote about it felt so immersive, I assumed it was something she knew firsthand. But, when I asked her about it, she laughed.

"I asked my best friend, 'Would you like to go on a little trip to Kentucky with me?'" she said. *"My husband was like, 'Do what you gotta do.'"* Leaving the husbands behind, the two spent a weekend touring distilleries, soaking in the history, and learning everything they could about bourbon. *"I left there a total convert,"* she admitted. *"Now, if I'm out, I'll always opt for an Old Fashioned."* The setting isn't just a backdrop, it's the heart of the story, adding to the romance.

I mentioned to Victoria during our conversation just how much I loved that her heroine saved herself. There were no dramatic, drawn-out moments where she was left helpless, she took control of her own fate. *"I was having fun with the idea of a heroine saving herself,"* Wilder said. And it wasn't just a one-off decision. Her books intentionally flip expectations within the romance genre.

 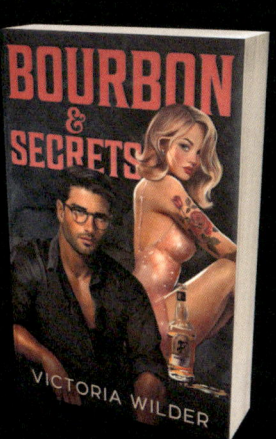

"In *Bourbon & Lies*, the heroine saves herself," she told me. "In *Bourbon & Secrets*, the hero saves her. As for the third book… Well, we'll have to wait and see what happens."

During our conversation, Wilder opened up about the realities of indie publishing; the creative freedom, the risks, and the smart investments that separate a hobby from a career. *"I knew I had to put my money into the right things,"* she explained. *"A great editor and an amazing cover designer, those two things sell books."* She was right. *Bourbon & Lies* was the breakthrough, her first book to generate enough revenue to reinvest in future projects. The distinctive covers of the **Bourbon Boys** series are the work of designer Loni Carr, known for her business The Whiskey Ginger. Now a full-time author, Wilder approaches writing with discipline. She structures her days with focused sprints alongside other authors, tracking word counts and staying accountable.

"You have to treat writing like a job," she said. *"Waiting for inspiration won't get books finished."*

With *Bourbon Proof* coming soon, Wilder is fully focused on her writing. But her impact as an indie author is already stretching far beyond what she imagined.

We saw it firsthand when we walked into Ivy & Ink, a brand new romance indie bookstore in Gold Coast, Australia. And there, sitting on the shelf, was *Bourbon & Lies*. Thousands of miles from where it was written, in a small independent bookshop on the other side of the world, Wilder's book had found a new audience. We already own a copy. We've already read it. But of course, we bought it again, because seeing an indie romance author's work travel so far, crossing oceans and landing in a bookstore halfway across the world, is something worth celebrating.

"It's amazing to see so many people opening bookstores and working directly with authors," Wilder said. *"It's changing the game for indie writers."*

And she's right. Indie bookstores aren't just stocking books, they're championing authors, hosting events, and bringing readers closer to the writers they love.

If you're a romance reader and haven't picked up a Victoria Wilder book yet, now's the time. Her storytelling is sharp, her characters unforgettable, and her books impossible to put down. She's an author on the rise, and if I had to bet on the next big indie name, my money's on her.

So here's to great books, great bourbon, and an author whose rise is just getting started. 🥃🥃

Want to keep up with Victoria Wilder?
Follow her on Instagram **@authorvictoriawilder.**
and check out her latest releases!

THE BOOK THAT BRINGS YOU BACK

There's a moment every reader knows, that spark, that shift, when a book grips you so tightly that you forget you ever stopped reading in the first place.

Maybe, life got busy, maybe the days blurred into work, responsibilities, and endless scrolling; maybe you told yourself you weren't a reader anymore, but then, it happens.

It's different for everyone. A novel that hooks you from the first line. A story so vivid it pulls you out of your own world and into another. A character you can't stop thinking about. A memoir that speaks to your soul. A self-help book that changes the way you see things. It's that book, the one that brings you back.

We hear it all the time. People say they "used to love reading," but somehow, it slipped away. And yet, when the right book finds them, it changes everything. The pandemic reminded us of this. When the world paused, people turned back to books. And when the power goes out, when the Wi-Fi is down, when there's nothing else to do but sit in the quiet, reading finds us again.

The truth is, everyone can be a reader. Some just haven't met the right book yet. But once you do, once a story grabs you, there's no going back. Suddenly, you're staying up too late turning pages, looking for the next book that will make you feel this way again.

Books are patient. They wait. And when the time is right, they welcome you home.

So, if you've drifted away from reading, or if you've never been much of a reader, don't worry. That book is out there. The one that will remind you why stories matter, why words can change everything. And when you find it, you'll wonder how you ever went without.

Because there is a book out there for everyone. You just have to find it.

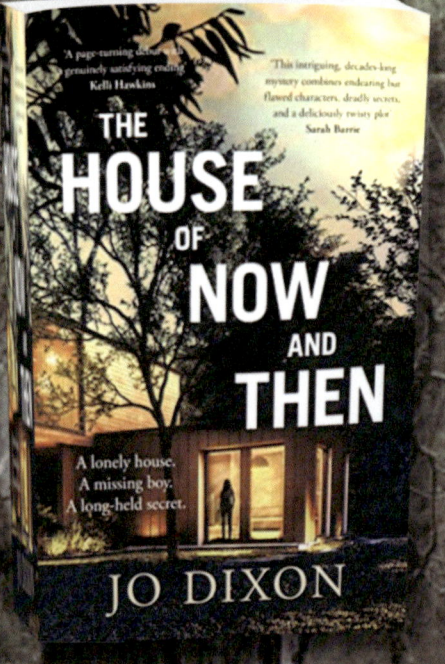

I wasn't expecting *The House of Now and Then* to hit me the way it did, but Jo Dixon absolutely delivered. This book sucks you in, builds tension beautifully, and keeps you flipping pages late into the night. It's a slow unraveling of past and present, where you start out thinking you know what's happening—only to realize you don't.

Told across two timelines, the novel follows a woman trying to escape her past in a secluded Tasmanian house and a group of friends in 1986 whose summer takes a dark turn. At first, the stories seem unrelated, but Dixon weaves them together, twisting their connections in ways you won't see coming.

And the villains?—awful, heinous—the kind of characters you love to hate. They feel disturbingly real, which only makes them worse. But, the protagonist in the present timeline was my favorite. She is flawed, lost, and struggling to move forward, but by the end, I felt completely connected to her.

Dixon also nails the setting—the Tasmanian landscape is more than a backdrop, creating the sense of eerie isolation that lingers long after the last page is turned—and that ending? Let's just say I didn't see it playing out quite like that. There were clues, but Dixon still managed to throw in surprises that made me rethink everything.

If you love mystery, suspense, and stories packed with deep emotional layers, this one is for you. It's not a fast-paced thriller, but it's gripping, atmospheric, and absolutely worth the read.

★ ★ ★ ★

Verdict: A suspenseful, immersive mystery that stays with you.

Book Review!

Photo credit: Jo Dixon's Tasmanian backyard

In Conversation with
Jo Dixon

We reached out to Jo Dixon about *The House of Now and Then*, and she shared this insight into her writing journey:

"This story started as two very different ideas, a road trip gone wrong and a woman escaping to an isolated house in Tasmania. At some point, they merged, and the house became the thread tying past and present together. I nearly gave up on this book many times, but the characters wouldn't let me. They kept filling my head, demanding to be heard. So, I returned to the keyboard, determined to get it right."

It wasn't always mystery and suspense for Dixon—she originally tried writing romance. The problem? She couldn't help killing off her characters. *"I kept adding dark backstories, scheming manipulators, and twisty surprises,"* she admitted. It turns out, she wasn't bad at writing, she was just writing in the wrong genre.

That perseverance paid off. After years of hard work, Dixon's debut landed her a two-books deal with HarperCollins. After *The House of Then and Now*, she followed it up with *A Shadow at the Door* in 2024, and her third novel, *A Disappearing Act*, will be out this October. With the fourth book already in progress, it's clear the stories and the characters aren't done with her yet.

BookTok
BOOKSTAGRAM

Trending Now

BookTok and Bookstagram are thriving online communities on TikTok and Instagram, bringing readers together through a shared love of books. These platforms have transformed the way people discover and engage with literature, with visually captivating content and heartfelt recommendations driving reading trends and boosting book sales.

They've become go-to spaces for uncovering new reads and sparking viral book moments, reshaping how readers connect with stories and each other.

BOOKWORLD.CLUB

Contemporary Romance

"First-Time Caller" by B.K. Borison

- Aiden Valentine, host of Baltimore's late-night romance hotline, has lost faith in love, until a young caller seeking dating advice for her single mother, Lucie, changes everything. Their unexpected connection sparks a viral moment, forcing Aiden and Lucie to rethink love and second chances.
- **Why it's trending**: This heartfelt romance, inspired by Sleepless in Seattle, has charmed readers with its warmth, humor, and swoon-worthy moments. Fans love Borison's ability to blend nostalgia with fresh, feel-good storytelling.

"Deep End" by Ali Hazelwood

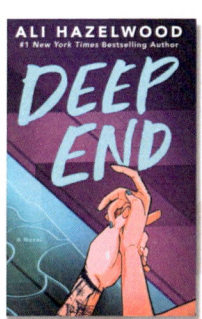

- Stanford junior and platform diver Scarlett Vandermeer is focused on medical school and recovering from a career-threatening injury. Her disciplined routine is disrupted when a secret connects her with swim captain and world champion Lukas Blomqvist, leading to a steamy, unexpected relationship.
- **Why it's trending:** This book has sparked major conversation, with readers passionately debating its mix of swoon-worthy romance, sports drama, and emotional depth. Whether they love it or critique it, everyone is talking about it.

Mystery/Thriller

"Listen for the Lie" by Amy Tintera

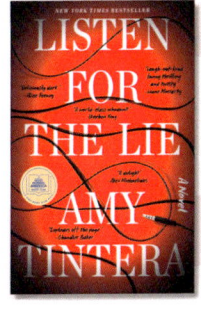

- Five years ago, Lucy was found wandering her Texas hometown, covered in her best friend Savvy's blood, with no memory of that night. Though never charged, the town believes she's guilty. Now, true crime podcaster Ben Owens revisits the case, prompting Lucy to return home to uncover the truth about what happened to Savvy.
- **Why it's trending:** Tintera's adult debut masterfully blends suspense with dark humor, offering a fresh take on the true crime genre. Readers are captivated by Lucy's sharp, witty narrative and the novel's insightful critique of media sensationalism.

Historical Fiction

"Broken Country" by Clare Leslie Hall

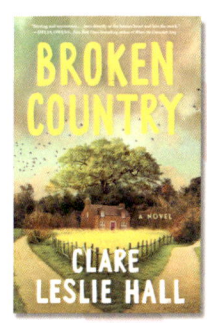

- In 1968 Dorset, England, Beth and her husband Frank lead a quiet life on their sheep farm, still mourning the tragic loss of their young son. Their fragile peace is disrupted when Gabriel Wolfe, Beth's first love, returns to the village with his son, Leo. As old passions rekindle and buried secrets resurface, Beth finds herself torn between her past and present, leading to deadly consequences.
- **Why it's trending:** Selected as a Reese's Book Club pick for March 2025, "Broken Country" has captivated readers with its blend of suspense and emotional depth. Clare Leslie Hall's masterful storytelling and the novel's unexpected twists have made it a standout choice among book clubs and literary enthusiasts.

Dark Romance

"Caught Up" by Navessa Allen

- Nico "Junior" Trocci, entrenched in a world of violence, rekindles his obsession with Lauren Marchetti, a woman he once deemed unattainable. As their paths cross in a play club, their flirtations intensify, challenging boundaries and igniting a dangerous passion.
- **Why it's trending:** As the anticipated sequel to the viral TikTok sensation "Lights Out," this novel delves deeper into dark romance themes, captivating readers with its morally complex characters and intense narrative. Note: "Caught Up" is scheduled for release on 10 June 2025.

KRISTI & JENN - TWO BOOKENDS

There's something special about The Two Bookends. Jenn and Kristi aren't just best friends, they're the kind of best friends everyone hopes to have.

The ones who know your worst moments and love you through them, who have stood beside you in your biggest life moments, who passed you tissues when life got hard. The ones who laughed with you in high school, raised kids alongside you, and still find new ways to make life fun decades later.

They were passing notes to each other in eighth grade, and now they're passing books back and forth, proving that some friendships only get better with time. In 2022, this next chapter of their friendship began with a single book. Jenn picked up a Colleen Hoover novel, looking for an escape, and suddenly every book became a never-ending book swap. What had been a monthly catch-up turned into weekly book trades, buddy reads, and endless conversations about stories that made them laugh, swoon, and cry.

Books didn't just bring them closer together—they gave them something to hold onto. When life felt overwhelming, stories gave them an escape. Soon, they weren't just reading more; they were searching for more—more books, more recommendations, more people who loved stories as much as they did. And that's when they found BookTok and Bookstagram.

It wasn't smooth sailing at first. They were below beginner influencer level. *"We didn't know how to turn off filters or edit videos for months. What are we doing here? Do we even know what we're doing?"* They fumbled their way through it, but it never felt like work. It was just an excuse to hang out even more. *"Hey, we both finished this book, come over so we can film our review."*

That's the part that stuck. The joy of sharing books with your best friend—not just talking about them, but laughing, reacting, and experiencing them together. Along the way, they connected with other readers, favorite authors, and people who just got them.

There's a Jane Fonda quote about the power of female friendships that sums them up perfectly.

"I have my friends, therefore I am. They make me stronger. They make me smarter. They make me braver. They tap me on the shoulder when I might be in need of course correcting."

Jenn and Kristi's friendship is exactly that. Books didn't start their bond, but they deepened it. Reading together became another way to show up for each other—to escape, to laugh, to feel. And, as their community grew, it became something bigger: proof that books aren't just about what's inside them—they're about who you share them with.

They found their first real BookTok obsession with Kate Stewart's *Ravenhood series*—a series so good, they had to talk about it. Then came Meghan Quinn. Last year, they picked up her *Vancouver Agitators series*, and within a week, they were hooked—the humor, the chemistry, the absolute fun of it—it was an instant fandom moment. From there, they moved straight into her *Bridesmaid for Hire* series, and now they never miss a Meghan Quinn release.

Their football commentary reaction video went viral with 21 million views and more than 15,000 shares because, let's be honest, hearing football commentators talk about "thrusting" and "sucking in balls" with a bookish mindset is comedy gold.

Kristi's recent birthday winery tour was another highlight—Coyote Ugly-style dancing, singing, filming hilarious videos, and, of course, plenty of wine. But it wasn't just a party. It was a mix of lifelong friends they'd pulled into reading and fellow influencers and authors they'd met through the book world. Matching tattoos to commemorate the trip, 'Why not?,' because when books bring you together, it's for life.

With so many Bookstagram accounts, what makes them stand out? You're not just watching one person review books—you're watching two best friends tease each other, burst into laughter mid-sentence, and keep it real. Whether they're glammed up or in pajamas with messy hair, they show up exactly as they are. It feels like hanging out with your book-loving besties. They aren't about tracking goals or ranking books; they read for the pure joy of it. As they say, "*Not every book is for every person, but there is a person for every book.*"

They also don't tear books down—no negative reviews, no trashing authors—just celebrating the stories they love and helping readers find their perfect match. That's the kind of energy we need more of in the book world.

While their love for books and their community is obvious, they've never let it take over their lives. Family and friendship always come first. They fit BookTok around their lives—not the other way around; maybe that's why their content never feels forced, because they're here for the joy, connection, and love of books, not for the pressure.

They've also gone from fangirling over authors to actually talking with them. They've started hosting Instagram lives with authors, bringing their bookish discussions full circle. It's one thing to read a book you love—it's another to chat with the person who wrote it, and now they get to do that regularly.

TOP READS 2024

1. *The Vancouver Agitators* Series by Meghan Quinn;
2. *Bridesmaid for Hire* by Meghan Quinn;

3. *Catch the Sun* by Jennifer Hartmann;
4. *Older* by Jennifer Hartmann; and
5. *Severed Heart* by Kate Stewart.

  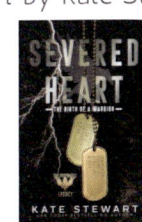

If you're heading to a book event, you might even see them in person. They'll be at Wild and Windy Chicago in May 2025, SpicyReads in San Diego (June 2026,) and Heathens and Heartbreakers Book Bash in Texas (June 2027.)

MOST ANTICIPATED READS THIS YEAR

- *Mr. Prescott* by TL Swan;
- *Entwined* by Rebecca Quinn (final book in the Brutes of Bristlebrook series);
- *Bridesmaid by Chance* by Meghan Quinn;
- *Brimstone* by Callie Hart;
- *One Golden Summer* by Carly Fortune; and
- *Dream On* by Jennifer Hartmann.

Their daughters have grown up as best friends too, proving that some friendships are meant to last generations.

If you're not following them yet, do yourself a favor and do so, because Jenn and Kristi don't just talk about books—they make you want to love reading even more. They remind you why books bring people together, why stories matter, and how sharing them with your best friend makes everything better.

Penny for My Thoughts

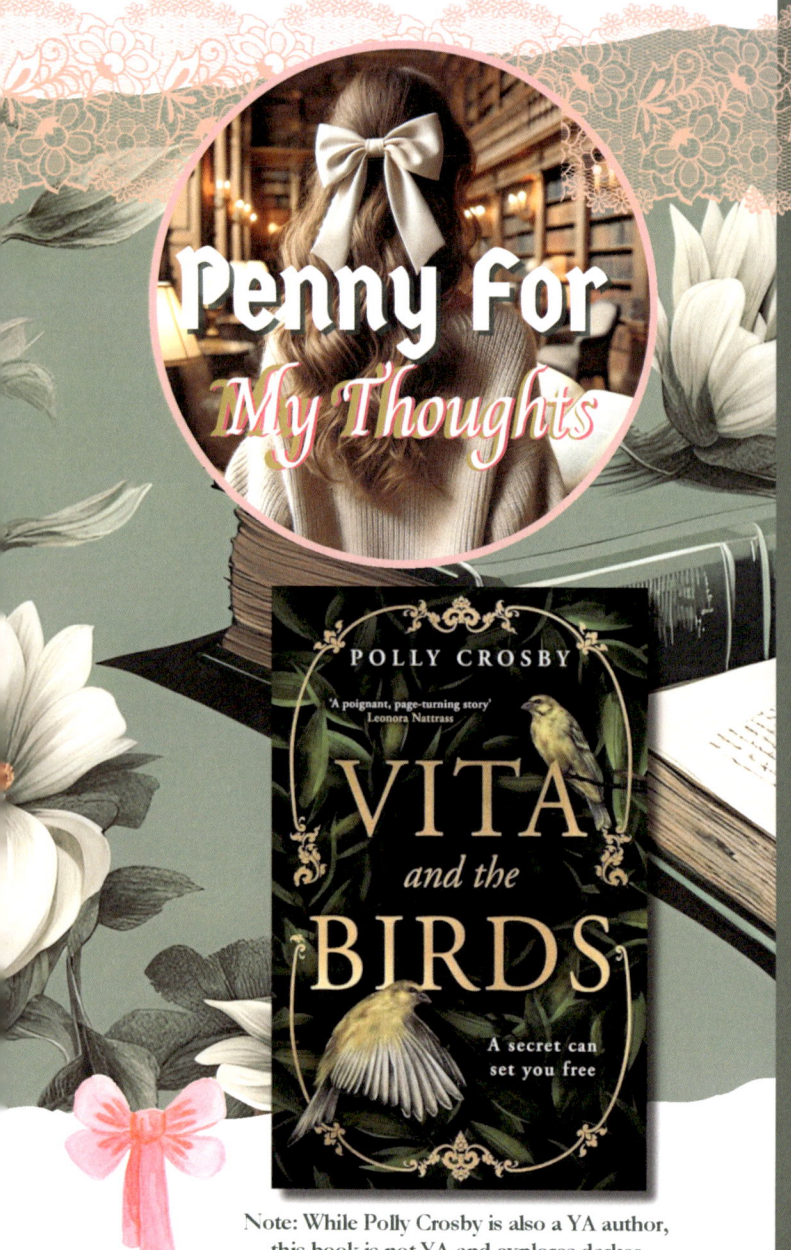

VITA AND THE BIRDS
Polly Crosby

This was the most beautiful book, one of my absolute favorites. The writing style is so descriptive and Crosby has done an amazing job with the development.

This book is so stunningly descriptive, has such an incredible plot, and a beautiful mix of dark academia and gothic settings. Add in the complexity of the characters and as I've already mentioned, the SUPER WELL DONE foreshadowing, this story is beautiful in every way shape and form.

This book is a soul crushingly gorgeous and gut wrenchingly amazing portrayal of transformative grief, showing how love changes people, and how family is so important.

Note: While Polly Crosby is also a YA author, this book is not YA and explores darker themes.

Penny's Y.A. Shelf

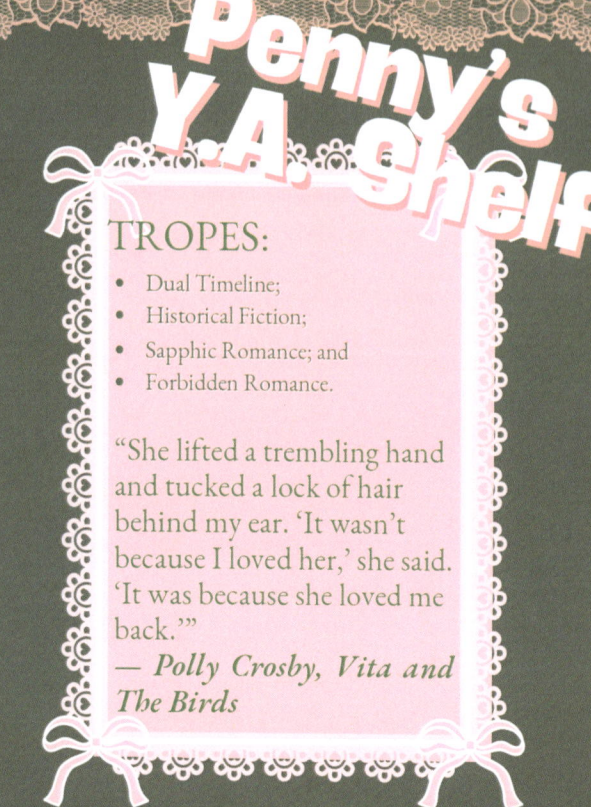

TROPES:
- Dual Timeline;
- Historical Fiction;
- Sapphic Romance; and
- Forbidden Romance.

"She lifted a trembling hand and tucked a lock of hair behind my ear. 'It wasn't because I loved her,' she said. 'It was because she loved me back.'"
— *Polly Crosby, Vita and The Birds*

I've had a really wonderful year with the number of bookish opportunities I've been given lately—I can't help but feel so excited for the year ahead! I have opportunities to read some arcs from some really incredible authors (genuinely, I'm so excited to share some of them with you all!) and already some of them have been truly amazing.

It's also given me the chance to chat with some authors and connect with a few of them, and really get to know them! But it means I get to offer you something really cool and that's on the next page—enjoy my gift to you!

I've slowed down quite a lot on my reading during this time of year—school will do that to you—and whilst I'm still significantly ahead on my goal of 75 books for 2025, I'm definitely missing how much I was able to read earlier in the year. I mean I went from 21 books in January to five in February.

I miss reading. How are you going with your book goal?

Speaking of book goals, do you have any non-book-count-related goals for the year? Last year one of my goals was to expand the amount of genres I read, and whilst that's still in there a little bit (not that I've made any progress—it's been all romance and fantasy books for me this year so far) my main goal for 2025 is to get some special editions of my favorites and start annotating my other copies. Let me know what you think or any goals you have!

Signing off, Penny xx

An Interview with Polly Crosby - Vita and the Birds

Q & A

Pen: "Hi, I was wondering if I could ask you a couple of questions about VatB?"

Pol: "Hi! Of course!

Pen: "Oh, my goodness great thank you! So first off, I guess I'd really like to ask what would be your inspiration for the Cathedral of the Marshes? It seems like a super unique setting!"

Pol: It's loosely based off The Winter Gardens at Great Yarmouth. The name in my novel comes from a very grand church in Suffolk nicknamed the Cathedral of the Marshes.

Pen: Ooh, that's super cool! I'll definitely be looking up pictures.
Pen: Would you say there are any songs that remind you of VatB?

Pol: I know there are a lot of authors who listen to music while writing, but I need silence or white noise! Something classic, a little haunting and a bit gothic would fit.

Pen: Interesting! Would you say there were any books you read to get inspiration for it?

Pol: Books that inspired me: *Jane Eyre*, *I Capture the Castle*, *The Offing*, to name a few!

Pen: I'm over here taking notes... Book recommendations galore!
Pen: Who would you say your favourite character is?

Pol: Not quite sure about favourite character. Leo is the closest to me, I think. I probably love Dodie the best because she sees people in a way I wish I could.

Pen: What made you pick canaries as Vita's main bird association over another bird species?

Pol: I'm not sure! I think I knew they had to be a caged bird and the golden colour of them fitted with the opulence.

Thank you, Polly, for your time.

MEET NIKITA
THE BOOK DRAGON YOU NEED TO KNOW

If you're a book lover, you need Nikita on your radar. She's not chasing follower counts, trying to be an influencer, or treating books like a business. She's here because she loves books completely, obsessively, and unapologetically.

But here's the twist: If you saw her incredible book collection, filled with rare editions and stunning special releases, you'd think she'd been a lifelong collector. That's not the case. Nikita grew up reading, but life got in the way —kids, full-time work, running a household. Reading took a backseat. Then, one day, she picked up a book, and everything changed.

It all started with library loans. Then came the discovery of special editions. Before she knew it, she was hunting down collector's copies, tracking exclusive releases, and stacking books faster than she could find space for them. Her collection has outgrown the bookshelves, the crates, and possibly her patience, but not her love for the hunt. Right now, her books are tucked into every available corner of the house. She has shelves in her daughter's room, a bookcase in the bedroom, another tiny one squeezed into a nook, and

boxes of books downstairs. But, if you ask her? "I'm just waiting for my kids to move out."

Nikita doesn't just read, she tears through books at a pace that leaves most people in the dust. Audiobooks are her secret weapon, and she listens at speeds that would make your head spin. She's the kind of reader who finishes a book before you've even decided what to read next. Naturally, this led her into A.R.C. (advanced reader copy) reviewing, where her sharp eye and honest takes earned her a reputation with authors and publishers alike.

Her thoughtful, insightful reviews didn't just catch the attention of book-lovers, Amazon took notice, too. They invited her to Amazon Vine, an exclusive program where top reviewers receive free products in exchange for honest feedback. "I could grab a 3-D printer, but I'd rather save money on dishwasher tablets," she jokes, proving that even in a sea of perks, she keeps it practical.

One of the best things about Nikita? She's not just in this for herself—she's here to lift others up. She's built real friendships through books, including her now close connection with indie author T. J. Maguire. What started as a simple online interaction turned into a true friendship, and now? Nikita helps with admin, emails, and the occasional book signing.

She's also connected with readers worldwide. One of her book friends, Aaron, lost his husband, and they bonded over sending each other books. That's their love language—not constant messages, just the quiet exchange of stories. Another friend is going through cancer treatment, and they swap recommendations to keep each other going. She's not here for drama, just to support authors and connect with people who love books as much as she does.

There are plenty of people in the book world, but Nikita is different. She's real, passionate, and endlessly supportive. She's the kind of person who will send you a book just because she knows you'll love it. She's carved out a place for herself in the book industry without even meaning to—just by being herself. And if you ask her what's next? Well, she's still eyeing that full-house library. Her husband might need to start getting comfortable in the shed.

Want book recs, collector's editions, and a book bestie who gets it? Follow Nikita on Instagram!

@nikita.bookshelf

<u>Favourite genre:</u> Fantasy.

<u>Top author:</u> Danielle L. Jensen.

<u>How she reads:</u> Audiobooks.

<u>Unique challenge:</u> Top five books/series you would take in case of an house fire.

<u>Current reads:</u> Rose in Chains A.R.C.

<u>Special interests:</u> Gardening—growing heirloom varieties of fruit and vegetables (the dream is to one day own a farm and live off the land) which we do now on a small scale.

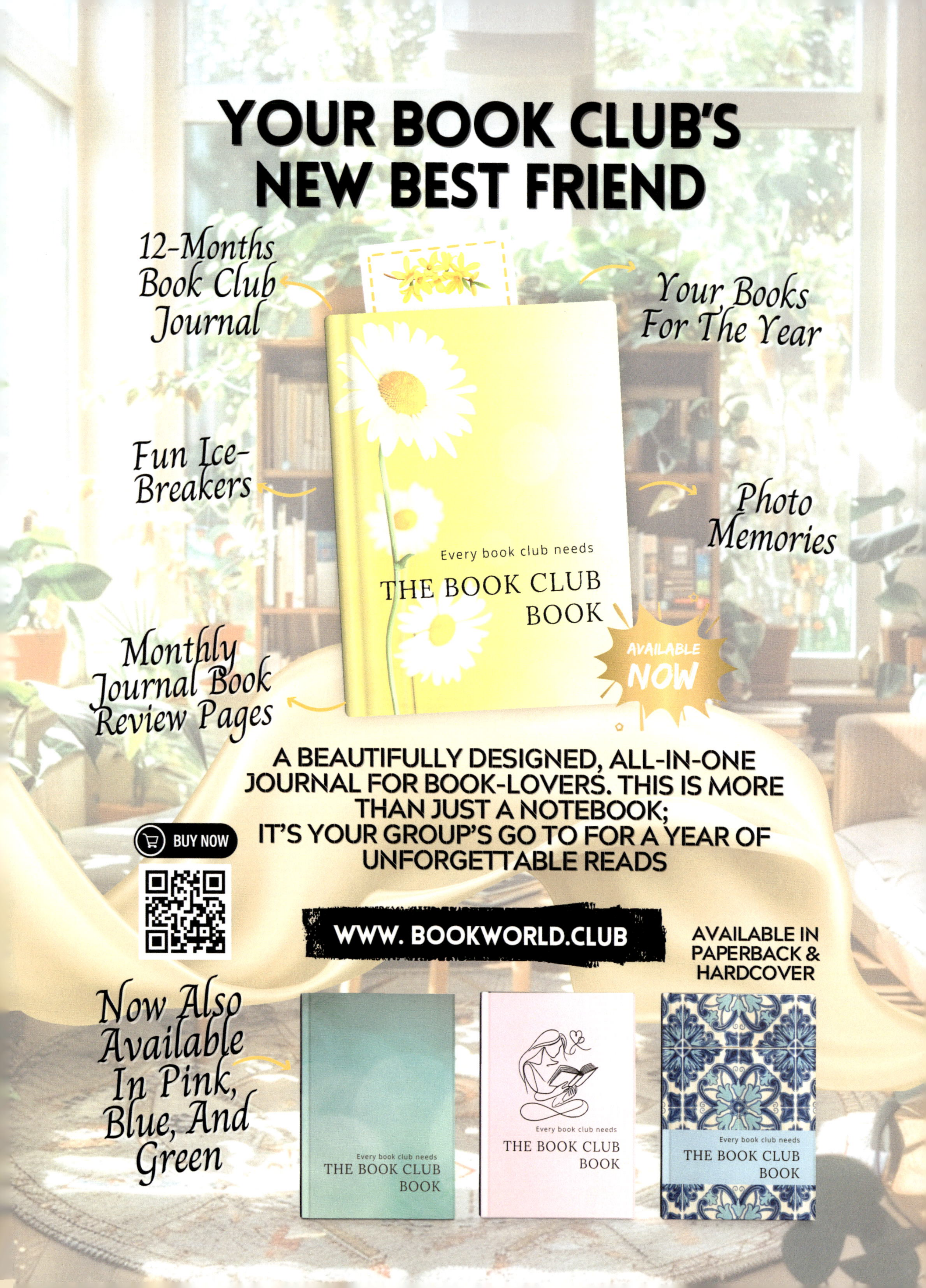

YOUR BOOK CLUB'S
NEW BEST FRIEND
12-Months Book Club Journal
Your Books For The Year
Fun Ice-Breakers
Photo Memories
Every book club needs
THE BOOK CLUB BOOK
Monthly Journal Book Review Pages
AVAILABLE NOW
A BEAUTIFULLY DESIGNED, ALL-IN-ONE JOURNAL FOR BOOK-LOVERS. THIS IS MORE THAN JUST A NOTEBOOK; IT'S YOUR GROUP'S GO TO FOR A YEAR OF UNFORGETTABLE READS
BUY NOW
WWW. BOOKWORLD.CLUB
AVAILABLE IN PAPERBACK & HARDCOVER
Now Also Available In Pink, Blue, And Green
Every book club needs
THE BOOK CLUB BOOK
Every book club needs
THE BOOK CLUB BOOK
Every book club needs
THE BOOK CLUB BOOK

We love book clubs. But, we also know that, sometimes, planning the perfect book club night takes more effort than you have time for.

That's why we created Book World Club Guides so you can spend less time organizing and more time enjoying the book with friends.

Our guides take the guesswork out of planning, giving you ready-to-go ideas that make your book club experience effortless.

✨ **Stuck for ideas?** We've got you covered.
🍷 **Need a themed recipe?** It's in there.
🎲 **Want a fun game?** Done.
💬 **Discussion questions?** Ready to go.

Each guide is designed to bring something extra to your book club something fun, something easy, something that makes the night even better.

And if we don't have a guide for your book yet? Just ask! We'll make one for you.

Let's make book club the easiest and best part of your week.

Download your guide today!

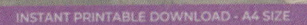

Fireside Stories

The Fireside Family Book Club That Has Become A Legacy

Book clubs come and go. Life gets in the way, people move, schedules fill up, and what once felt so important quietly fades into something of the—but not this book club. This one is different. This is a family book club, and this November will mark their twenty-third anniversary. No matter what life has thrown at them, Fireside has remained.

It all started with Aunt Val. She is the heart of Fireside Book Club, the founder, the historian, the one who takes notes like a courtroom stenographer, ensuring no moment is lost. In 2002, she had an idea: Let's start a family book club. A handful of women—sisters, a mother, a daughter, an honorary aunt—all loved the idea, and on 5 November 2002, they held their first official meeting. They gathered at Aunt Val's house, near the fireplace, and unknowingly created something that would last for decades. Seats were claimed that night and without realizing it, they became permanent. For 22 years, those seats, whether physical or virtual, have remained theirs.

Life changed, as it does. Anitra was just 19 when the book club started, a sophomore in college. Over the years, she graduated, moved across the country, got married, and built a life of her own in Las Vegas. Other members moved too, Florida, Texas, California, even Germany—but the books kept them together. Before Zoom, there were emails, handwritten letters, even D.V.D.s, recorded and mailed, filled with book reviews. Aunt Val, the club's official historian, would read every word aloud, ensuring no one's voice was left unheard. Babies were born, careers shifted, life went on, but Fireside stayed.

At their 15-years anniversary, Fireside celebrated in a way only they could by connecting with the authors who had shaped their journey. Aunt Val took the lead, reaching out to writers whose books had left a mark on them over the years, and the response was overwhelming. Letters poured in, filled with personal messages* from authors who were touched by Fireside's dedication to reading. It was a moment

*See a short selection on back cover

Fireside Book Club
Est. 5 Nov. 2002

In a family where books matter, so do traditions.
The rules of Fireside are simple.

- **Miss three books in a row?** You better have a **very** good excuse.
(*Not that it's ever happened—no one wants to be left out!*)
- **Pick a seat at the first meeting?** That's **yours for life**. No take-backs. No switching.
- **Every month, a name is drawn from the trinket box.** That person picks three book choices, and the club votes. **Democracy**—just with strong opinions.

And then there are the **unspoken rules**:

- **Never question Aunt Val's note-taking skills.** She's the **keeper of history**, capturing every book, every discussion, and every special moment so that no memory is ever lost.
If there's a dispute? The records don't lie.
- **Bees are always welcome.** Their first book, *The Secret Life of Bees*, became more than just a story. Now, every time they see a bumblebee, it's a quiet reminder of where they started.

that solidified what Fireside had become: not just a book club, but a living, breathing history of their family.

As Aunt Val so perfectly put it:

> "Here's the big problem: I feel a bond with each and every book, good, bad, or so-so. I am savoring each written review from our out-of-state members especially, and feel like Book World Magazine could do a series on us as these archives are proving to be immensely sentimental. Each author that sent us messages on our fifteenth anniversary touched me so, and how do you single out just a few? I write you now with tears in my eyes and a lump in my throat knowing it is impossible for me to share the wonder that is The Fireside Book Club."

Then came Covid in 2020. And for the first time in 18 years, Fireside fell silent.

They had already felt the weight of loss—Aunt Jeanne passed in 2018, but the club carried on, gathering as they always had. Then, in 2022, they lost Grandma. She wasn't just a member; she was a force. Their sassy, not-your-typical grandma, who had shaped their love of books and stories from the very beginning. This time, the silence felt final. Fireside, without her, seemed impossible.

But in this club, no one is ever truly gone. Aunt Val kept their names in the trinket box. When one is drawn, the club picks from their past book suggestions, ensuring their presence is always felt. Their books still get read. Their voices still matter. And when those books are chosen, it feels like they're still there, sitting in their seats, discussing the story alongside everyone else.

After two years without meetings, it was author Kim Fay who unknowingly brought them back together. She and Anitra connected after Anitra shared her thoughts on *Love & Saffron* online. As they talked, Kim learned about Fireside Book Club—its history, its traditions, and the way it kept loved ones present through stories. Moved by what she heard, she made a simple offer: *"Read my book, and I'll join your discussion."*

That Zoom call could have been a farewell. Instead, it was a rebirth and the beginning of a beautiful friendship.

> ❝ There are definitely books we have loved more than others —but it's the discussions that really are what we love the most. ❞
> — *Anitra*

Since then, the book club has been back in full swing. The traditions remain. The same conversations, sometimes passionate, sometimes hilarious, still happen. And now, a new generation is waiting for their turn. Anitra's stepdaughter Carmen at 18 is eager to join. Isabelle is counting down the days until she's old enough. Because in this family, reading together isn't a hobby. It's a legacy.

For years, they joked: *Maybe one day, someone would hear about them. Maybe their story was special enough to be shared.* We believe it is. Fireside Book Club is more than just a book club, it's a testament to family, tradition, and the power of stories. We feel privileged to be the first to share it.

In a world where families drift and book clubs fade, Fireside remains. Because books don't just bring them together. They keep them together. And the fire has never gone out.

Tenth Anniversary

Aunt Val's program for the tenth anniversary included this intro and a beautiful cake to celebrate!

OVER THE LAST TEN YEARS....

We've traveled together on this Good Earth, walking through Tallgrass, down The Road, the Red Hook Road, just Outside Valentine. We've been held captive in a Room, searched for The Shack and contemplated A Dive from Clausen's Pier, or a Skinny Dip at Empire Falls, while listening to Beach Music on our trek to the Norwegian Wood. We walked together, never in Total Control, but never Left Neglected. We felt a kinship with The Book Thief and The Book Borrower. We feared for The Kite Runner and The Historian's plights and were fearful of The Collector. Knowing they had No Second Chance, our hearts ached and broke for The Hatbox Baby, The Last Child, The Girls and The Stolen Child. We braved Angels and Demons and fought alongside Abraham Lincoln Vampire Hunter on The Darkest Evening of the Year. We've cheered, and maybe envied, the courage of The Girl With the Dragon Tattoo.

After ten years, not much will Shock us, we already know the Secret Life of Bees and What the Dead Know. But with The Help of our fellow Fireside Book Club Members, we'll share new and exciting reads. And we'll do what we do best... Talk, talk...

83 books and counting!

Fireside's Favorite Books

The Secret Life of Bees by Sue Monk Kidd
The Historian by Elizabeth Kostova
The Good Earth by Pearl S Buck
The Stolen Child by Keith Donohue
The Book Thief by Markus Zusak
Abraham Lincoln: Vampire Hunter by Seth Graham-Green
The Snow Child by Eowyn Ivey
A Man Called Ove by Fredrik Backman
Love and Saffron by Kim Fay
Remarkably Bright Creatures by Shelby Van Pelt
All the Colors of the Dark by Chris Whitaker

Fireside Book Club est. 2002

We are the Fireside Book Club
Book reading is our goal
Be it tome or thinner
Loser or winner
We discuss and critique them all

Poem by Grandma Esther
2003

An Ode to Aunt Val

Aunt Val is the keeper of stories, the heart of Fireside, the unwavering force that has held this book club together for more than two decades. She ensures that no voice, no opinion, no moment is ever lost. More than just its founder, she has created a space where family bonds are strengthened, where books are not just read but lived.

Her dedication is quiet but fierce, her love for this club as deep as the stories they explore. Because of her, every member—past, present, and future—has a place in Fireside. Even those who are no longer here still have a seat at the table, their book picks waiting in the trinket box, their presence felt in every meeting. Fireside is more than a book club; it is a family tradition, a legacy of love and literature, and at the centre of it all is Aunt Val—the woman who made sure everyone always has a place by the fire.

www.ingramcontent.com/pod-product-compliance
Lightning Source LLC
Chambersburg PA
CBRC091723070526
44585CB00008B/160